119

About this book

The Sixties is often referred to as the decade when young people became the centre of attention. It was a time when teenagers openly questioned the values and way of life of their parents and the Establishment. The hippy movement was born out of this discontent, and hippies preached the ideals of love and peace to counteract the materialism and greed they saw in much of the world around them.

In this book Susan Cleeve shows how the changes in the world of fashion and pop music reflected the underlying social changes. When the Beatles burst on the pop scene they seemed to express so much of what young people were feeling. They shocked people with their long hair, and the arrival of the mini skirt on the fashion scene caused even more of a stir. But gradually it was noticed that even parents were beginning to grow their hair a little longer and wear their skirts a little shorter!

The events and personalities of the Swinging Sixties are vividly brought to life through the words and pictures of this book.

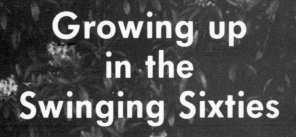

Growing up
in the
Swinging Sixties

SUSAN CLEEVE

1980
96p.
illus

Wayland

(series: Growing Up in Other Times)

Growing up in Other Times

Frontispiece: Sir Matt Busby and Bobby Charlton lead young footballers on to the field

ISBN 0 85340 755 X

Copyright © 1980 Wayland Publishers Ltd

First published in 1980 by Wayland Publishers Ltd,
49 Lansdowne Place, Hove, East Sussex, England, BN3 1HF

Text set in 12 pt. VIP Univers by Trident Graphics Limited,
Reigate, Surrey
Printed and bound in Great Britain
at The Pitman Press, Bath

Contents

1 News Headlines

The 1960s are often called the Swinging Sixties in Britain because that was the time when pop music became more than just something you listened to. It became a way of life for the young. With the arrival of the Beatles on the pop scene in 1962 Britain took over from America as the centre of the pop world.

There was a revolution in the fashion world. Young men changed their formal suits for jeans. They grew their hair long until at the end of the decade it was often shoulder-length. Girls everywhere started wearing mini skirts or jeans. 'Pirate' radio stations pumped non-stop music into people's homes. Suddenly young people seemed to have more money and freedom than they had ever had before and were determined to make the most of it. And although parents snorted disapprovingly, even their own skirts became a little shorter and their hair a little longer! As the Sixties moved on, young people really did change the character of the decade.

But not everything in the Sixties was 'swinging', and in this first chapter we shall look at some of the serious events which made the headlines. Many of these events were to change young people's lives far more in the long run than all the swinging things which seemed so important at the time.

The picture opposite shows the launching of Apollo 11 from Cape Kennedy on 16th July 1969.

Princess Margaret marries The Sixties
began with the fairytale wedding of Princess Margaret to Anthony Armstrong-Jones in Westminster
Abbey on 6th May 1960. It was a perfect spring
day and the Princess travelled in the famous glass
coach, watched by millions in the streets and on
television. In the picture you can see other members of the Royal Family. Few people would have
believed then that the couple would divorce in 1978.

The thalidomide tragedy Between 1958 and 1961 a drug called thalidomide was given to some pregnant women, which resulted in their babies being born with limbs missing. Some were born without arms, some without legs, and a few poor babies without either. They had stumps or flaps of skin where the limbs should be. This six-year-old girl has no arms, and her feet are almost directly joined to her pelvis. She needs artificial arms and legs to lead as normal a life as possible. There were over four hundred thalidomide victims in England alone. They are now in their early twenties.

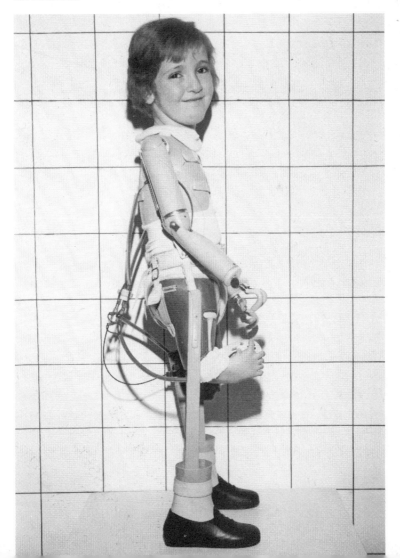

First man in space The Space Race between America and Russia began at the end of the Fifties. The Russians were first to launch a satellite, and were also first to send a man into space. He was cosmonaut Major Yuri Gagarin, who was launched into space in *Vostok 1* on 12th April 1961. He beat the American astronaut, Alan Shepard, by only three weeks.

The Cuba Crisis In 1962 the world hovered on the brink of nuclear war. The Communist country of Cuba, which lies only three hundred kilometres off the coast of America, had allowed Russia to build nuclear rocket launching sites in Cuba which were capable of bombing America. The Americans realized what was happening when U.S. airforce planes returned with this photograph showing the missile bases. President Kennedy warned President Khrushchev that ships suspected of carrying missiles would be stopped and searched. More Russian ships approached Cuba, and the American navy moved in. The world held its breath. Would the Russians stop, or would the Americans have to use force? Eventually the Russian ships turned round, and the missile bases were later dismantled.

The Great Train Robbery In the early hours of 8th August 1963 an armed gang of thirty masked men ambushed this Glasgow-to-Euston express train. They escaped with 120 mailbags, containing £2½ million. Several of the robbers received long prison sentences for their crime, but one of them, Ronald Biggs, is still free in Brazil, and many were never caught.

M 30204

EXTRA

PRESIDENT SLAIN

Texas Assassin Hits Kennedy in Automobile

News Call Bulletin
SAN FRANCISCO'S EVENING NEWSPAPER

Volume 5, No. 90   FRIDAY, NOVEMBER 22, 1963   Phone EX 7-5700   Price 10c

Mystery
San Carlos
Gun Battle

DALLAS---President John F. Kennedy is dead. He died after an assassin fired on his car leading a motorcade into Dallas, third stop on his Texas tour.

DALLAS (UPI)—President John F. Kennedy and Gov. John B. Connally of Texas were cut down by an assassin's bullets as they toured downtown Dallas in an open automobile today.

Death of Kennedy
The whole world was stunned by the news of John F. Kennedy's assassination. The young and popular President of the U.S.A. was shot in Dallas on 22nd November 1963 by Lee Harvey Oswald (who was himself shot before his trial). Kennedy was the fourth American president in a hundred years to die at the hand of an assassin.

Death of Sir Winston Churchill

On 24th January 1965 one of the greatest men in Britain's history died. He was Sir Winston Churchill, the man who led Britain to victory during the dark days of the Second World War. He was the first commoner since Gladstone to be given a state funeral and thousands of mourners filed past his coffin. He was mourned by people all over the world. In the picture Churchill's coffin on board HMS *Havengore* leaves Tower Pier for Waterloo. From there his body travelled by train to his chosen resting place in Bladon churchyard, Oxfordshire, where his mother was buried.

The Vietnam War One of the clouds which hung over the Sixties was the Vietnam War. Communist guerrillas (known as Viet Cong) with aid from Communist North Vietnam and Russia were trying to seize control of South Vietnam. Fearing the spread of Communism in Asia, America supported the South. Early in 1965 President Johnson ordered the bombing of military targets in North Vietnam. Despite protests against the war, American troops were sent over to help the South Vietnamese. By 1968 there were half a million American soldiers fighting in Vietnam. Here you can see soldiers carrying one of their injured men back to base. The war raged throughout the Sixties and peace was not achieved until the Seventies.

England won the World Cup

On 30th July 1966 English football history was made when England won the World Cup 4–2 against West Germany at Wembley. The feeling in the country afterwards has been compared with that of the celebrations after the Second World War! Everyone had 'world cup fever' and the triumphant team – Bobby Moore (Captain), Bobby and Jack Charlton, Geoff Hurst, Nobby Stiles, Martin Peters, Gordon Banks, Alan Ball, George Cohen, Ray Wilson and Roger Hunt – became schoolboy heroes. Here the team hold high their captain and their prized trophy.

The Six-Day War

In June 1967 the long war between Egypt and Israel flared up again. The Arab states of Egypt, Jordan, and Syria declared war on Israel. However, the Israeli army, directed by Moshe Dayan, won the war in only six days. Israel won much land from the Arab states, and for the first time in nearly 2,000 years the whole of Jerusalem was under Jewish rule. In the picture overjoyed Israelis welcome home their victorious troops.

Dr Martin Luther King

Combining his Christian principles with non-violent political action, Martin Luther King inspired the civil rights movement in America. He campaigned for black people to enjoy the same rights as white people, and not to have to live in special areas with their own buses, schools and cinemas. He led many peaceful marches to gain support for this cause. Here is Dr Luther King, with his wife, on his way to serve a five-day prison sentence for his involvement in a civil rights march in 1963. He was awarded the Nobel Peace Prize in 1964. Just four years later he was assassinated in Memphis.

Peace marches The 1960s was a great time for peaceful protest marches. The Campaign for Nuclear Disarmament (C.N.D.) was very active. Each year they held an Easter walk from Aldermaston in Berkshire (where there was an atomic weapons research establishment) to London. Men, women and children, and even babies in prams, would set out towards Trafalgar Square, but many of them dropped out with blistered feet before they reached it. Another campaign which had much popular support was against American involvement in the Vietnam War. Here is a group of young people demanding that the U.S. troops come home.

Student riots

There were student troubles throughout Europe and the U.S.A. during the Sixties. But it was the French students' revolt in May '68 which hit the headlines. The riots started as a protest against conditions at Nanterre University, outside Paris, and led to a general strike which nearly resulted in the downfall of the French Government led by President de Gaulle. There were battles between students and police on the campus. On Monday 13th May a tremendous demonstration marched through Paris with the students in the lead, supported by workers' organizations. Students seized their university buildings; workers seized their factories. Both strikers and students wanted to bring the Government down. However, in the elections of June 1968 the Gaullists won with an overwhelming majority.

Investiture of the Prince of Wales

The Queen named her son, Charles, Prince of Wales when he was only nine, and promised to present him to the Welsh people when he came of age. Prince Charles interrupted his studies at Cambridge to learn Welsh so that he could speak in Welsh at the ceremony. The Queen presented her son and heir to the Welsh people at a splendid ceremony at Caernarvon Castle on 1st July 1969. This is a very old custom dating back to Edward I who made his son the first Prince of Wales.

Man lands on the moon

America wanted to land a man on the moon before the end of the Sixties. They did it with five months to spare! On 20th July 1969 Neil Armstrong of the Apollo II mission stepped on to the moon. The landing was

shown on television and people all over the world heard Armstrong's historic words 'One small step for a man, one giant leap for mankind' from a quarter of a million miles away. The picture shows Edwin Aldrin setting up an experiment on the moon.

2 Fashions, Freaks and Fads

When people talk of the Swinging Sixties or Swinging London they refer to the period from 1964 when England became the centre of young fashion. Boutiques sprang up everywhere, and Carnaby Street and Kings Road became *the* places for 'with-it' teenagers. Union Jacks appeared on everything from carrier bags to cars. It was the age of bell-bottom jeans, skinny rib jumpers, mini skirts, knee-high boots, Mods and Rockers, hippies, and Flower Power.

Mary Quant (shown opposite) was more responsible for changing fashion trends in the Sixties than anyone else. She invented the mini skirt and introduced tights to Britain. These were very necessary with the arrival of the mini skirt. She designed clothes especially for young people, and brought fashionable clothes within the price-range of modern teenagers.

The Sixties was also a time of great social change. Many young people criticized the ideas and way of life of their parents and the Establishment. In their struggle to find their own identity, and create an alternative society, many of them turned to drugs. In search of new and exciting experiences they experimented with heroin and LSD, often with tragic results. Many stars of the Sixties – for example, Brian Jones of the Rolling Stones – died as a result of taking drugs.

Mods and Rockers

Rockers liked only rock-and-roll music and wished they could turn the clock back to the late Fifties when rock-and-roll had been all the rage. Both the boys and their girl-friends wore metal-studded leather jackets and rode motorbikes. Their image was 'tough'.

Mods, however, dressed in the latest fashion, loved dancing and rode scooters. Their image was 'trendy'. Sometimes there were clashes between rival groups of Mods and Rockers. Some of the ugliest of these took place on Brighton beach in 1964. On one occasion a youth was killed in a

deckchair-throwing, bottle-swinging session.

Over the years the Mods faded and Skinheads took their place, and Rockers turned into Greasers. Today we have punk rockers who seem to be a mixture of the two.

In the picture opposite two Mod girls sit on their boyfriends' scooters while the boys mill around. Scooters were very important to Mods and they decorated them with as many wing mirrors, badges, stickers and fancy back-rests as possible.

The picture above shows a Rocker and his girl both wearing leather jackets and looking 'tough'.

Ten Pin Bowling This craze was brought to
Britain from the U.S.A. Here is the first bowling
centre to open in Britain (January 1960) in Stam-
ford, North London. The biggest bowling centre in
the country was The Princess Bowl, Dagenham,
with twenty-four lanes, which opened in 1961. The
bowling alleys were open all day and evening and
people of all ages would come to play or watch.
There are only a few bowling centres left in the
country now as the game is much less popular.

The 'Wet Look' Who would have thought that oilskin (or PVC), usually associated with cycling capes and fishermen's gear, would ever be high fashion? Mary Quant did, and soon every fashion-conscious girl was wearing her 'wet look' raincoats and sou'westers. This outfit is called Christopher Robin (after Winnie the Pooh's friend). It is unusual because, although it is belted at the front, it buttons at the back.

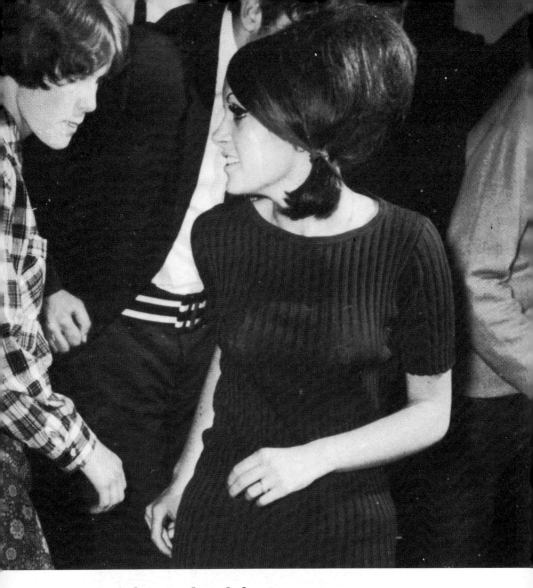

Backcombed hair In the early part of the decade girls backcombed their hair to make it stand high on top of their heads. The fashion lasted until about 1965. This teenage girl has backcombed her hair and is wearing the heavy eye make-up which was popular at the time. In the early Sixties trousers became acceptable as smart fashion for women, and hipster trousers were all the rage.

Cosmetics This was the new look make-up in the middle of the 1960s. Mary Quant made make-up less of a serious business and more of a fun art. Even the names she gave her products were new and amusing – 'Jeepers Peepers' for eye make-up, 'Starkers' for foundation and 'Blush-baby' for powders and rouges. The craze at this time was for dark, rather plummy colours – not only for lips, but for eyes too!

Unisex This word described clothes or hairstyles that could be worn by boys or girls. The 'little boy lost' look shown opposite was popular in the mid-Sixties. Girls wore their hair cropped short like a boy's and wore trousers with shirts, waistcoats and wide 'kipper' ties. Sometimes skinny rib jumpers were worn with the trousers. These were short and tight – almost as if an adult was wearing a child's jumper. This outfit is from Mary Quant's 'Ginger Group' range.

Boutiques These mini-skirted girls are in a boutique which was once a number 131 London bus. It was called 'Birds Paradise'. The catch phrase for girls at this time was 'birds' or 'dolly-birds' and the dresses designed for them were known as dolly dresses (as you can see they are rather like little girls' dresses). The straight one on the left is called a 'shift'. Other well-known boutiques were Quant's 'Bazaar', 'Biba' and 'Bus Stop'.

Face-painting This teenager looks as if she wonders if she dare go out with this Valentine's Day make-up. Face-painting was a fairly short-lived fad of 1967, influenced by Flower Power. She wears the long, straight hair and pale lips of the period and has 'eyelashes' painted in with eyeliner below her lower lashes — which was model Twiggy's hallmark.

Macrobiotic foods It was in the late 1960s that the great craze for brown rice, unprocessed flour and other macrobiotic foods began. These are foods that have been grown and prepared without the use of artificial chemicals, and are said to prolong life because of their health-giving properties. Many people grew their own, but they could (and still can) be bought in health food shops and good vegetarian restaurants. The picture shows shelves in a health store, displaying such foods and books on the subject.

Hippies and Flower Power The world-wide hippy movement was originally based in California and was largely formed as a reaction to American involvement in the Vietnam War. Many hippies expressed their contempt for society and its values by 'dropping-out'. The key words of the hippy movement were 'love' and 'peace', and they

hoped to create a world where war would be no more. However, they alienated most of society who disapproved of their long hair, scruffy appearance and use of drugs. The picture shows hippies engaged in the peaceful activity of blowing bubbles — the two policemen obviously wonder what it is all about!

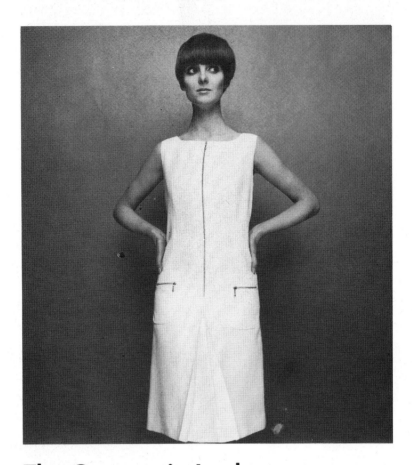

The Geometric Look

There was a great craze for black and white clothes in the Sixties, which grew out of 'op art' (patterns of optical illusions in black and white). It was known as the geometric look, and Vidal Sassoon, top hairstylist of the times, created a style to go with the clothes. Like them it was very simple in shape and very stark. The model in the white dress wears the 'geometric' cut, as does Mary Quant at the beginning of this chapter.

Although she designed mainly fun clothes Mary Quant also designed some couture dresses (exclusive, expensive clothes), like this black dress with the black ruff and roses — called Columbine.

3 The Beatles and the Pop Scene

Before the arrival of the Beatles on the pop scene in 1962 nearly all the top pop artistes had been American. 'Beatlemania' hit the country in 1963 – wherever the Beatles went they were followed by crowds of screaming, crying, fainting girls! The Beatles were probably the strongest influence on the development of pop music in the Sixties. They shocked people with their long hair! Their collarless jackets and button-down shirts started a new trend in men's clothes. Groups that came after them copied their four-man line-up and began writing their own songs which was almost unheard of in pre-Beatle days.

Flower Power was expressed in the gentle, slightly hypnotic music such as the Beatles' song 'All You Need is Love', which was released in 1967.

Little more than a year later the mood had turned 'psychedelic'. The term was first used to describe experiences derived from taking drugs, especially LSD. The Beatles' LP, *Sergeant Pepper's Lonely Hearts Club Band*, contained mostly psychedelic songs, and groups like Pink Floyd and The Moody Blues were also known for them. Later the word came to mean anything highly coloured, imaginative and trendy. There were psychedelic clothes, boutiques, record covers – and John Lennon even had a psychedelic Rolls-Royce!

The Beatles The Fab Four from Liverpool –
George Harrison, Paul McCartney, John Lennon
and Ringo Starr – brought a new sound and mood to
pop music and drew the young of many nations
together. Most of their songs were written by Paul
and John. Their first hit was 'Love Me Do' in 1962,
and from then on until their break-up in 1970 they
had several hits a year. They made three films,
and formed their own record company called
Apple. By the time they were awarded MBEs in
1965, they were all millionaires.

Brenda Lee The tiny American girl with the big, big voice began singing in public at the age of three! She made her first record when she was just nine years old and a few years later had her first hit with 'Sweet Nothin's'. Even as a child she had the voice of a woman and would belt out rock songs as if she were twice the age. Brenda Lee remained successful right through the early Beatle days, and had twenty-two hit records between 1960 and 1965.

Rise of discos Discos are not new. They were brought over from France in the early Sixties – the word 'disco' is short for the French *discothèque*. The first disco opened in London in 1961. A disco is a dance hall where the music is

provided by records selected by a disc jockey, instead of live groups. The Twist was probably the first dance to hit the discos in 1961. Here is a group of twisting teenagers from the film *Don't Knock The Twist.*

The Rolling Stones They burst on the scene when people were just getting used to the Beatles and made them seem like tidy, short-haired angels by comparison! The Stones were raucous, ugly, scruffy and anti-everything, and yet they were adored by their fans. They have been called the best rock group ever. The Stones' early music was based on the Negro rhythm-and-blues music. They look very different here, in 1963, from the way they look now. From left to right: (top) Bill Wyman, Mick Jagger and Charlie Watts, (centre) Brian Jones, who died in 1969, and (bottom) Keith Richards.

Cilla Black Liverpudlian Cilla (whose real name was Priscilla White) was one of Brian Epstein's Mersey Sound. These included other pop artistes such as The Beatles and Billy J. Kramer who all came from the River Mersey area of Liverpool and were managed by Brian Epstein. Girl singers found 1964 was their lucky year. Lulu, Sandie Shaw and Cilla Black all had several hits that year. Cilla's infectious giggle and friendly personality on her television shows (this picture is from one of them) made her popular with all ages.

Lulu Pint-sized Marie McDonald McLaughlin Lawrie from Glasgow bounced on to the television screens as Lulu with a hit record, 'Shout'. It was 1964 and she was just fifteen years old. This is Lulu and her backing group, The Luvvers, on a BBC2 pop programme, *The Beat Room*.

Sandie Shaw

The story goes that Sandra Goodrich, a punch card operator from Dagenham, hid in a hamper in the dressing room of pop star, Adam Faith, and sprang out and sang to him. If it is true she must have impressed him for Adam Faith later became her manager. Sandie usually sang barefoot and many girls wanted to look like her and copied her clothes and hairstyle. She won the Eurovision Song Contest in 1967 with the song, 'Puppet On A String'. Here Sandie is a guest in an Iron Curtain country. The uniformed gentleman is obviously amazed at the shortness of her dress!

Pop Concerts and Festivals Open air
pop concerts flourished in the Sixties. In 1969 a
quarter of a million Stones' fans gathered in Hyde
Park, London, to listen to their idols. This free con-
cert served as a tribute to Brian Jones who had
died a few days earlier in his swimming pool,
already ill as a result of taking drugs. Mick Jagger
released 2,000 white butterflies in his memory and

as a symbol of peace. The biggest pop festival of
all time was at Woodstock, just outside New York,
when half a million young fans came for three
days to listen to top groups like The Who and Jimi
Hendrix Experience. A film was also made of the
event.

This picture shows the Rolling Stones at a con-
cert at Longleat in 1964.

The Beach Boys This American group competed with the Beatles throughout the Sixties for top position on the pop charts in Britain and the U.S.A. Their 'surfing' sound was as unique as the Beatles' Mersey sound and for many years the

race was close, though finally the Beatles pipped them to the post internationally. Here are the Beach Boys, from left to right: the three Wilson brothers, Carl, Brian and Dennis, and Mike Love and Al Jardine, in their very early days in 1965.

The Who They were the great heroes of the Mods and their songs seemed to say all that teenagers felt, particularly 'My Generation', released in 1965. It was amazing to watch 'Mad' Moon frantic on drums, Pete Townshend smashing his guitar, and exciting lead singer, Roger Daltrey. Townshend wrote their rock opera 'Tommy' in the Sixties, but it was not staged or filmed until the Seventies. The Who (minus Keith Moon, who died from an overdose of drugs in 1978) are still a popular band, but very different from how they appeared below in 1965. From left to right: Pete Townsend, Roger Daltrey, John Entwistle and Keith Moon.

Bob Dylan Young people in the Sixties hailed
Dylan as spokesman for the age. His voice
sounded a little like a gravel mixer, but he was a
song-writer of quite extraordinary talent, and each
one of his folk-songs had a message. 'The Times
They Are A-Changin' and 'Like a Rolling Stone'
became anthems of the time. 'A Hard Rain's A
Gonna Fall' was a warning about nuclear fall-out
and 'With God on Our Side' was an anti-war song.
Many people recorded Dylan songs — Joan Baez is
perhaps the best known of them all.

The Bee Gees Originally there were five members — the three English Gibb brothers, Barry, Robin and Maurice, and two Australians. Britain's Home Secretary tried to send the Australian members of the group home when their work permits ran out, but there was such an outcry amongst fans with processions to Whitehall that

the Home Secretary relented and they were allowed to stay. 'New York Mining Disaster, 1941' was the record that first got them into the British charts in 1967. The present Bee Gees group is made up of just the Gibb brothers – the ones in the front of the picture, left to right: Barry, Robin and Maurice.

Stevie Wonder

The blind Negro singer, Stevie Wonder, first had hit records at the age of thirteen. In a few years he had become the biggest name on the Tamla-Motown record label. He was originally known as 'little' Stevie Wonder, but had to drop the first part when he grew too tall! He sounded as if he sang each song from the heart, whether it was the romantic 'My Cherie Amour' or the joyful 'Uptight (Everything's All Right)', and accompanied himself on the piano and harmonica. He continued to record best-selling hits all through the Seventies.

Diana Ross and the Supremes Diana
Ross started her singing career as lead singer with
the original Supremes. The other two singers were
Cindy Birdsong and Florence Ballard. They began
singing at church gospel meetings, and eventually
became one of the most successful of the giant
Tamla-Motown groups. In 1967 alone they earned
seven gold discs and had twelve best-selling
albums. Diana Ross quickly earned the reputation
as the best female black rock singer, and left the
Supremes to become a solo singer. She has starred in two films, *Lady Sings the Blues* and
Mahogany.

4 Heroes and Heroines

Every age has its heroes, and the Sixties was no exception. The idols of the day were not only the usual ones – film stars and singers – but also disc jockeys, models and sportsmen. Radio disc jockeys (DJs) had not existed before the Sixties, but became teenage heroes as they broadcast pop music to fans from the illegal 'pirate' radio ships. Models had always been admired, but before the Sixties they were rather remote, unreal figures. However, the Sixties saw the arrival of a new type of model who appealed to young people because of their 'ordinariness'. Suddenly every teenage girl wanted to look like Twiggy or Jean Shrimpton.

In the Sixties footballers took on the status of film and pop stars, and boys dreamed of becoming football heroes like Bobby Moore, the Charlton Brothers, or George Best, whose earnings climbed to unbelievable figures for the time. Muhammad Ali became the highest paid and certainly the best publicized sportsman ever. With his quick, off-the-cuff sense of humour, his own big mouth was surely his best publicity agent.

Many of these idols lent their names to children's football and cricket games, sports equipment, books, ties and T-shirts, and children badgered their parents to buy these goods for them. The picture opposite shows Muhammad Ali singing with the Beatles just before he won the World Heavyweight Championship title.

Jimmy Saville OBE The ageless Jimmy Saville was a Top of the Pops disc jockey and had his own radio chat show, *Speakeasy*, on Radio 1. At one time he dyed his hair half black and half white and appeared for weeks like that on television. In this photograph he is wearing a Union Jack tie. In the late Sixties Union Jacks on clothes, badges and carrier bags were a great craze. But Jimmy Saville was not just a zany pop personality. He also did a lot of work for charity and it was for this that he was awarded the OBE. He now uses the title as part of his name.

Tony Blackburn The ever youthful Tony
Blackburn began his career as a disc jockey on
board the 'pirate' radio ship, Radio Caroline.
Before the British government brought out the
Marine Broadcasting Offences Act in 1967 to close
down the pirates, Tony Blackburn left. He was the
first disc jockey on the air when BBC Radio 1
opened in 1967. The gimmick of his shows has
always been his dreadful 'groan' jokes, like this
one:

'My uncle has just been given a knighthood.
It keeps his ears warm when he's asleep.'

Kenny Everett The extraordinary Kenny Everett was another disc jockey of the Sixties who joined BBC Radio 1 after the pirate station, Radio London, closed down. He was well known for speaking his mind but eventually went too far and had to leave the BBC. Nothing stops the bubbling Everett though and he now has his own television show, *Kenny Everett's Video Show* on Thames Television and a three-hour Saturday show on Capitol Radio.

Jean Shrimpton This is Jean Shrimpton, international model, and her photographer boyfriend, David Bailey, in 1963. Both models and photographers became trendy in the Sixties. 'The Shrimp', as she was known, had enormous eyes, very long legs and long hair, and her beautiful face stared out from the covers of the best fashion magazines of the Sixties. David Bailey himself became a world-famous photographer during these times.

Twiggy Daughter of a London carpenter, Lesley Hornby was spotted by a photographer outside her school gates and within six months had become a world-famous model. She was nicknamed Twiggy because she was stick-thin and weighed only six and a half stone. Suddenly every teenage girl wanted to be thin. Her appeal lay in her 'ordinariness' and teenage girls everywhere identified with her. Here is Twiggy in 1967 at Madame Tussauds, London, with a plaster copy of herself. The very short hair, mini skirt and knee-high boots are typical of the year's fashions.

Bobby Moore Robert Frederick Moore became one of the biggest names in English football during the Sixties. He joined West Ham at the age of seventeen and later became their captain. He was the youngest ever Footballer of the Year when he was twenty-three, and won more caps than any other English footballer. He captained the victorious England team in the 1966 World Cup, and was made Sportsman of the Year. In 1967 he was awarded the OBE and, after sixteen amazing years with West Ham, moved to Fulham.

The Charlton Brothers
Fiery Jack Charlton (right) and his quieter, younger brother Bobby (left) were both football heroes of the Sixties. 'Big Jack' played for Leeds United and Bobby played for Manchester United. They were both schoolboy apprentices to their clubs and signed on as professionals when they were seventeen. Bobby Charlton, a former Schoolboy International, was one of the eight survivors when the Manchester United chartered plane crashed in Munich in 1956, killing nine members of the team. The brothers are best known for being members of the winning England side in the World Cup at Wembley in 1966.

Muhammad Ali

'I'm the prettiest fighter' and 'I'm the greatest', claimed Muhammad Ali and so he was! He was born as Cassius Clay in 1942 in the U.S.A., and changed his name to Muhammad Ali when he became a Muslim. He won the World Heavyweight title from Sonny Liston in 1964. The picture shows Ali beating George Chuvalo in 1966.

In 1967 the American government took his boxing licence and title away when he refused to be drafted into the U.S. army on religious grounds. He was out of boxing for three years. Then he tried to regain his title, but found he was not fit enough. However, he did win it back in 1974. He has a marvellous sense of fun, and wrote this poem predicting in which round his opponent would fall:

> 'When you come to the fight
> Don't block the halls,
> And don't block the door,
> For y'all may go home,
> After round four.'

George Best Although much admired as a footballer, and swooned over for his good looks, Best's failure to turn up for training sessions and his sudden disappearances earned him a reputation for being unreliable. His footballing skills were undisputed though – he started playing for Northern Ireland when he was only seventeen, and won thirty-seven international caps. He later played for Fulham and for Manchester United, and was in the United team when they became the first English club to play in the European Cup in 1968. He also owned a disco and a men's boutique in Manchester in the Sixties. George Best now plays in the U.S.A.

Omar Sharif Omar Sharif was born Michael Shalboub in Egypt in 1932. Because of his dark good looks and flashing eyes, he was usually cast in the role of romantic lover. Amongst his many films were *Lawrence of Arabia, Mayerling* and *Dr Zhivago.* In this photograph Omar Sharif plays the Russian doctor, with Julie Christie as Lara, in *Dr Zhivago* in 1965.

Sean Connery He was much better known as James Bond, or agent 007. Bond is the Super Spy who always wins. Sean Connery played the original Bond (Roger Moore now takes the role), beginning in 1962 with *Dr No* and ending with *Diamonds are Forever* in 1971. He left the Bond films to try and change his image, but is still thought of as James Bond the First. This is Connery, as James Bond, in *Diamonds Are Forever.*

Michael Caine

Michael Caine was a new type of film hero. The characters he played had working-class backgrounds, similar to his own, and he never disguised his south London accent. Caine's best films were *The Ipcress File, Funeral in Berlin,* and *Billion Dollar Brain*. In all these films he played Harry Palmer, the Cockney answer to James Bond. Here he is in *Alfie* which was released in 1966. The doll on the mantlepiece is a gonk. There was a great craze for gonks in the early Sixties.

5   Screen and Print

The development of the media in the Sixties was probably one of the most important trends of the decade. The term 'media' refers to the means by which people communicate – for example, television, radio, newspapers, advertising.

All sorts of people who in the Fifties had just been people doing their jobs became 'personalities' in the Sixties. Newsreaders, interviewers and sports commentators suddenly became well-known names. The best known of these was David Frost, who was unheard of in 1960, but by 1969 had become one of the most famous television personalities on both sides of the Atlantic.

Shows, books, musicals, films and television series all influenced the way in which people dressed, spoke and lived. The media turned sport, and especially football, into another form of show-business.

The picture opposite shows some of the magazines which sprang up during the decade, including *What's On, Time Out* and *Private Eye.*

That Was The Week That Was

Satire was a very popular form of humour in the Sixties. It began with *Beyond the Fringe* (a stage show), and was followed by *That Was The Week That Was* (affectionately known as TW3). This late night Saturday show was a satirical revue which looked back on the week's happenings. It shocked some and delighted others, as the BBC had never before presented satire and jokes about the monarchy and religion. Here is compere David Frost with some of his team — William Rushton, Millicent Martin, Roy Kinnear and Lance Percival. The show first appeared in 1962 and was last seen at the end of 1963.

Juke Box Jury This programme in fact began in 1959 and was a completely new idea. The show's host was David Jacobs (now better known for compering Radio 4's *Any Questions*). A team of four well-known guests would listen to newly released pop records and vote whether they would be hits or misses. This picture was taken in 1961 and singer Frankie Vaughan, Gloria de Haven, DJ Pete Murray and actress June Thorburn were on the panel. It was a highly successful show and ran until Christmas 1967. It was revived in 1979 with Noel Edmonds as host.

Dr Who *Dr Who* first appeared on television in 1963. It was a new idea to show science fiction stories for children. Many adults complained that the series was too frightening, but children loved being scared by Daleks and the Yeti. Four actors have played the part of Dr Who. The picture opposite shows the second of them, Patrick Troughton. The first doctor was played by William Hartnell, the third by Jon Pertwee and the most recent by Tom Baker.

Blue Peter *Blue Peter* actually began in 1958, but deserves to be mentioned here because it was consistently the most popular children's programme all through the Sixties. Here are presenters Valerie Singleton, Peter Purves and John Noakes with the four lion cubs 'adopted' by the programme in 1968. *Blue Peter* is still as popular as ever with its new presenters.

Top of the Pops

Top of the Pops never dies. It was first seen on BBC television in June 1964 and has scarcely been off the air since. The show was much the same then as now, except that some of the disc jockeys were different. Alan Freeman, Jimmy Saville or Simon Dee compered

the show in the Sixties. The picture shows Brian
Poole and the Tremeloes in 1964. The Top 20 chart
in the background includes names such as Cilla
Black, The Searchers, Cliff Richard, Jim Reeves,
Chuck Berry, Gerry and the Pacemakers, and — of
course — the Beatles!

The Forsyte Saga

This was the story of the troubles of a nineteenth-century family, based on the novels of John Galsworthy. The series was a tremendous success and the twenty-six episodes were shown on British television three times from 1966 to 1969. The serial was also televised in various countries around the world, including Russia. It starred (from left to right) Nyree Dawn Porter as Irene, Kenneth More as Jo, Joseph Conner as Jolyon, and Eric Porter as Soames Forsyte.

Summer Holiday This film came out in 1963 when Cliff Richard and the Shadows had already been big stars for five years. It was a carefree, happy movie about a group of teenagers who kitted out an old London bus for travel and took off on the holiday of a lifetime touring Europe. Here is Cliff in a song and dance routine from the film.

Help! This crazy adventure comedy was the Beatles' second film. Ringo's new ring turned out to be more than he had bargained for. When it became stuck on his finger, he discovered that he who wore the ring was next to be sacrificed to the Goddess Kaili. *Help!* follows the adventures of the Fab Four as they try to escape from the fanatical religious sect, headed by High Priest Clang. Here they are, in disguise, in the Austrian Alps in their attempts to evade the clan and save Ringo's neck. The film was followed by a novel and a very successful LP of the same name.

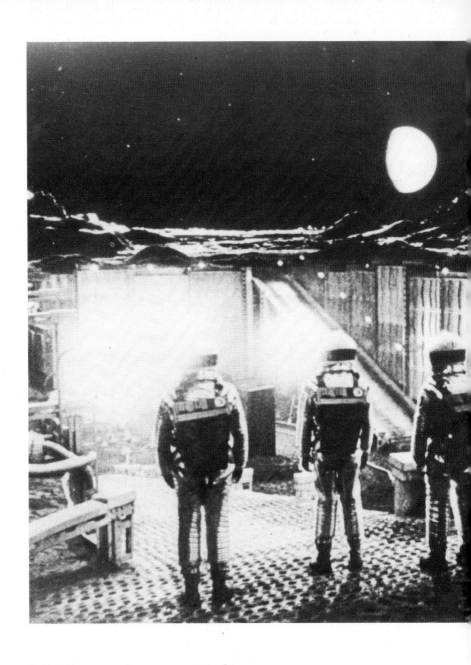

2001 – a Space Odyssey One of the best science fiction films ever made appeared in the Sixties. It is the year A.D. 2001 and American spacemen discover a strange obelisk on an uninhabited

planet. Intelligent beings must have put it there.
Soon they realize that the obelisk is watching
them, recording their behaviour, and sending
messages back to its masters.

Mary Poppins Mary Poppins was an amazing children's governess and nanny — perhaps the most magical thing about her was that she could fly! Here is Julie Andrews, who plays Mary Poppins, in the 1964 Walt Disney film with actor Dick Van Dyke and their animal friends. They have just stepped into one of his pavement drawings and made it come alive!

Pirate radio stations These were illegal radio stations which broadcast non-stop pop music to British listeners from ships anchored outside British waters. Before the 'pirates' there was no radio station which catered for pop (except for Radio Luxembourg which could only be heard in the evening). Radio Caroline was the first British pirate station, and boasted an audience of nine million listeners and disc jockeys such as Tony Blackburn. A few of the pirates were based on off-shore wartime forts.

In 1967 the government passed the Marine Broadcasting Offences Act which made pirate stations illegal. Most of them closed down soon after. However, on 30th September 1967 Tony Blackburn, a former pirate disc jockey, opened BBC's own pop channel, Radio One.

Comics and magazines

Many of the comics and magazines which were read in the 1960s are still on sale today. A copy of *Dandy* costs 6p today but in 1963 it only cost 3d (that is, just over 1p!). The stories in *Judy* never seem to change and are as popular today as when they began. The teenage magazine *Fabulous 208* which started in 1964 is still popular. 'Fabulous' or 'fab' was a slang word of the decade. Unfortunately, other teenage magazines have died out, including *Rave* and *Petticoat*. Fashion magazines like *19* and *Honey* are still going strong.

New Words

Blues	simple, rhythmic form of music which was originally the folk music of American slaves.
Boutique	a small shop which sells the latest fashion in clothes.
Cap	anyone who plays football, cricket or rugby for England is awarded a special cap.
Gold disc	award made to artistes whose records sell a million copies.
Gonk	a stuffed, round doll with a funny face, usually exceptionally ugly.
Hippy	member of a world-wide youth movement in the Sixties who preached the ideals of love and peace, grew their hair long and experimented with drugs.
LP	long-playing record.
Media	means of instant communication – for example, radio, television, films.
Peace march	a group of people marching to demonstrate their desire for an end to all war.
Personality	person who is famous, not for what they do, but for who they are.
Psychedelic	word which came to mean anything which is highly coloured, imaginative and trendy.

Rock music	type of pop music which grew out of the Fifties' rock-and-roll music.
Satire	type of humour which pokes fun at serious things.
Trendy	in the latest fashion.
Unisex	clothes or hairstyles which could be worn by either men or women.

Picture Acknowledgements

The author and publishers would like to thank all those who have given permission for copyright pictures to be reproduced on the following pages: Associated Press, 18; BBC, 48, 62, 63, 76, 77, 78, 79, 80–81, 82–3; CIC, 86–7; Dezo Hoffman Ltd., *jacket picture*, 42, 46, 49, 52–3, 56–7, 58, 59, 60; EMI, 84; Evening Argus, 26, 27; Keystone Press Agency, 20, 67, 68, 70; London Express, 15; London Features International Ltd., 43, 47, 54, 55, 64; Mary Quant Ltd., 24, 29, 30, 32, 38, 39; National Film Archives, 84, 85, 86–7, 88–9; Novosti, 10; Popperfoto, 8, 11, 14, 16, 17, 19, 21, 28; Syndication International, 30 33, 34, 42, 50–51, 65, 66; D. C. Thomson & Co. Ltd., 91; Western Americana Picture Library, 13, 69. All other pictures are from the Wayland Picture Library.

More Books

The Sixties: An Illustrated History in Colour 1960–1970, Nathaniel Harris (Macdonald).

The Illustrated History of Rock Music, Jeremy Pascall (Hamlyn).

When Pirates Ruled the Waves, Paul Harris (Impulse Publications).

Help! – the book of the film (Mayflower Books).

Beatles, The Singles Collection 1962–1970, (Wise)

Bob Dylan Himself, His Words and His Music (Duchess Music).

Quant by Quant (Cassell).

The Charlton Brothers, Norman Harris (Stanley Paul & Co.).

Bobby Moore, Jeff Powell (Everest Books).

Famous Names in Popular Music, Graham Rickard (Wayland).

A Laugh in Every Pocket, Tony Blackburn.

Record Hits: The British Top 50 Charts 1954–1976, Clive Solomon (Omnibus).

Ask at your local library for copies of magazines which appeared in the 1960s.

Index